Reports In American Newspapers-II

by

Swami Vivekananda

ABOUT THE AUTHOR

Swami Vivekananda was born Narendranath Datta in India on January 12, 1863. He died on July 4, 1902, and was the most important student of the Indian saint Ramakrishna. He was an important part of bringing Vedanta and Yoga to the West. He is also charged with making people more aware of other religions and making Hinduism a major world religion. Vivekananda had a lot of success at the Parliament. In the years that followed, he gave hundreds of lectures across the United States, England, and Europe to spread the main ideas of Hinduism. He also started the Vedanta Society of New York and the Vedanta Society of San Francisco, which is now the Vedanta Society of Northern California. Both of these groups became the basis for Vedanta Societies in the West. Vivekananda was one of the most important philosophers and social reformers in India at the time. He was also one of the most successful and powerful Vedanta missionaries in the West.People now think of him as one of the most important people in modern India and Hinduism. Mahatma Gandhi said that after reading Vivekananda's works, he loved his country a thousand times more.

CONTENTS

India: Her Religion And Customs

(*Salem Evening News*, August 29, 1893)

In spite of the warm weather of yesterday afternoon, a goodly number of members of the Thought and Work club, with guests, gathered in Wesley chapel to meet Swami Vive Kanonda, a Hindoo monk, now travelling in this country, and to listen to an informal address from that gentleman, principally upon the religion of the Hindoos as taught by their Vedar (Vedas.) or sacred books. He also spoke of caste, as simply a social division and in no way dependent upon their religion.

The poverty of the majority of the masses was strongly dwelt upon. India with an area much smaller than the United States, contains twenty three hundred millions [sic] of people, and of these, three hundred millions [sic] earn wages, averaging less than fifty cents per month. In some instances the people in whole districts of the country subsist for months and even years, wholly upon flowers (Mohua.), produced by a certain tree which when boiled are edible.

In other districts the men eat rice only, the women and children must satisfy their hunger with the water in which the rice is cooked. A failure of the rice crop means famine. Half the people live upon one meal a day, the other half know not whence the next meal will come. According to Swami Vive Kyonda, the need of the people of India is not more religion, or a better one, but as he expresses it, "practicality", and it is with the hope of interesting the American people in this great need of the suffering, starving millions that he has come to this country.

He spoke at some length of the condition of his people and their religion. In course of his speech he was frequently and closely questioned by Dr. F. A. Gardner and Rev. S. F. Nobbs of the Central Baptist Church. He said the missionaries had fine theories there and started in with good ideas, but had done nothing for the industrial condition of the people. He said Americans, instead of sending out missionaries to train them in religion, would better send some one out to give them industrial education.

Asked whether it was not a fact that Christians assisted the people of India in times of distress, and whether they did not assist in a practical way by training schools, the speaker replied that they did it sometimes, but really it was not to their credit for the law did not allow them to attempt to influence people at such times.

He explained the bad condition of woman in India on the ground that Hindoo men had such respect for woman that it was thought best not to allow her out. The Hindoo women were held in such high esteem that they were kept in seclusion. He explained the old custom of women being burned on the death of their husbands, on the ground that they loved them so that they could not live without the husband. They were one in marriage and must be one in death.

He was asked about the worship of idols and the throwing themselves in front of the juggernaut car, and said one must not blame the Hindoo people for the car business, for it was the act of fanatics and mostly of lepers.

The speaker explained his mission in his country to be to organize monks for industrial purposes, that they might give the people the benefit of this industrial education and thus elevate them and improve their condition.

This afternoon Vive Kanonda will speak on the children of India to any children or young people who may be pleased to listen to him at 166 North street, Mrs. Woods kindly offering her garden for that purpose. In person he is a fine looking man, dark but comely, dressed in a long robe of a yellowish red colour confined at the waist with a cord, and wearing on his head a yellow turban. Being a monk he has no caste, and may eat and drink with anyone.

* * *

(*Daily Gazette*, August 29, 1893)

Rajah Swami Vivi Rananda of India was the guest of the Thought and Work Club of Salem yesterday afternoon in the Wesley church.

A large number of ladies and gentlemen were present and shook hands, American fashion, with the distinguished monk. He wore an orange colored gown, with red sash, yellow turban, with the end hanging down on one side, which he used for a handkerchief, and congress shoes.

He spoke at some length of the condition of his people and their religion. In course of his speech he was frequently and closely questioned by Dr. F. A. Gardner and Rev. S. F. Nobbs of the Central Baptist church. He said the missionaries had fine theories there and started in with good ideas, but had done nothing for the industrial condition of the people. He said Americans, instead of sending out missionaries to train them in religion, would better send someone out to give them industrial education.

Speaking at some length of the relations of men and women, he said the husbands of India never lied and never persecuted, and named several other sins they never committed.

Asked whether it was not a fact that Christians assisted the people of India in times of distress, and whether they did not assist in a practical way by training schools, the speaker replied that they did it sometimes, but really it was not to their credit, for the law did not allow them to attempt to influence people at such times.

He explained the bad condition of women in India on the ground that Hindoo men had such respect for woman that it was thought best not to allow her out. The Hindoo women were held in such high esteem that they were kept in seclusion. He explained the old custom of women being burned on the death of their husbands, on the ground that they loved them so that they could not live without the husband. They were one in marriage and must be one in death.

He was asked about the worship of idols and the throwing themselves in front of the juggernaut car, and said one must not blame the Hindoo people for the car business, for it was the act of fanatics and mostly of lepers.

As for the worship of idols he said he had asked Christians what they thought of when they prayed, and some said they thought of the church, others of G-O-D. Now his people thought of the images. For the poor people idols were necessary. He said that in ancient times, when their religion first began, women were distinguished for spiritual genius and great strength of mind. In spite of this, as he seemed to acknowledge, the women of the present day had degenerated. They thought of nothing but eating and drinking, gossip and scandal.

The speaker explained his mission in his country to be to organize monks for industrial purposes, that they might give the people the benefit of this industrial education and thus to elevate them and improve their condition.

* * *

(*Salem Evening News*, September 1, 1893)

The learned Monk from India who is spending a few days in this city, will speak in the East Church Sunday evening at 7-30. Swami (Rev.) Viva Kananda preached in the Episcopal church at Annisquam last Sunday evening, by invitation of the pastor and Professor Wright of Harvard, who has shown him great kindness.

On Monday night he leaves for Saratoga, where he will address the Social Science association. Later on he will speak before the Congress in Chicago. Like all men who are educated in the higher Universities of India, Viva Kananda speaks English easily and correctly. His simple talk to the children on Tuesday last concerning the games, schools, customs and manners of children in India was valuable and most interesting. His kind heart was touched by the statement of a little miss that her teacher had "licked her so hard that she almost broke her finger". . . . As Viva Kananda, like all monks, must travel over his land preaching the religion of truth, chastity and the brotherhood of man, no great good could pass unnoticed, or terrible wrong escape his eyes. He is extremely generous to all persons of other faiths, and has only kind words for those who differ from him.

* * *

(Daily Gazette, September 5, 1893)

Rajah Swami Vivi Rananda of India spoke at the East church Sunday evening, on the religion of India and the poor of his native land. A good audience assembled but it was not so large as the importance of the subject or the interesting speaker deserved. The monk was dressed in his native costume and spoke about forty minutes The great need of India today, which is not the India of fifty years ago, is, he said, missionaries to educate the people industrially and socially and not religiously. The Hindoos have all the religion they want, and the Hindoo religion is the most ancient in the world. The monk is a very pleasant speaker and held the close attention of his audience.

* * *

(Daily Saratoga, September 6, 1893)

. . . The platform was next occupied by Vive Kananda, a Monk of Madras, Hindoostan, who preached throughout India. He is interested in social science and is an intelligent and interesting speaker. He spoke on Mohammedan rule in India.

The program for today embraces some very interesting topics, especially the paper on "Bimetallism", by Col. Jacob Greene of Hartford. Vive Kananda will again speak, this time on the Use of Silver in India.

Hindus At The Fair

(Boston Evening Transcript, September 30, 1893)

Chicago, Sept. 23:

There is a room at the left of the entrance to the Art Palace marked "No. 1 — keep out." To this the speakers at the Congress of Religions all repair sooner or later, either to talk with one another or with President Bonney, whose private office is in one corner of the apartment. The folding doors are jealously guarded from the general public, usually standing far enough apart to allow peeping in. Only delegates are supposed to penetrate the sacred precincts, but it is not impossible to obtain an "open sesame", and thus to enjoy a brief opportunity of closer relations with the distinguished guests than the platform in the Hall of Columbus affords.

The most striking figure one meets in this anteroom is Swami Vivekananda, the Brahmin monk. He is a large, well-built man, with the superb carriage of the Hindustanis, his face clean shaven, squarely moulded regular features, white teeth, and with well-chiselled lips that are usually parted in a benevolent smile while he is conversing. His finely poised head is crowned with either a lemon colored or a red turban, and his cassock (not the technical name for this garment), belted in at the waist and falling below the knees, alternates in a bright orange and rich crimson. He speaks excellent English and replied readily to any questions asked in sincerity.

Along with his simplicity of manner there is a touch of personal reserve when speaking to ladies, which suggests his chosen vocation. When questioned about the laws of his order, he has said, "I can do as I please, I am independent. Sometimes I live in the Himalaya Mountains, and sometimes in the streets of cities. I never know where I will get my next meal, I never keep money with me I come here by subscription." Then looking round at one or two of his fellow-countrymen who chanced to be standing near he added, "They will take care of me," giving the inference that his board bill in Chicago is attended to by others. When asked if he was wearing his usual monk's costume, he said, "This is a good dress; when I am home I am in rags, and I go barefooted. Do I believe in caste? Caste is a social custom; religion has nothing to do with it; all castes will associate with me."

It is quite apparent, however, from the deportment, the general appearance of Mr. Vivekananda that he was born among high castes — years of voluntary poverty and homeless wanderings have not robbed him of his birthright of gentleman; even his family name is unknown; he took that of Vivekananda in embracing a religious career, and "Swami" is merely the title of reverend accorded to him. He cannot be far along in the thirties, and looks as if made for this life and its fruition, as well as for meditation on the life beyond. One cannot help wondering what could have been the turning point with him.

"Why should I marry," was his abrupt response to a comment on all he had renounced in becoming a monk, "when I see in every woman only the divine Mother? Why do I make all these sacrifices? To emancipate myself from earthly ties and attachments so that there will be no re-birth for me. When I die I want to become at once absorbed in the divine, one with God. I would be a Buddha."

Vivekananda does not mean by this that he is a Buddhist. No name or sect can rebel him. He is an outcome of the higher Brahminism, a product of the Hindu spirit, which is vast, dreamy, self-extinguishing, a Sanyasi or holy man.

He has some pamphlets that he distributes, relating to his master, Paramhansa Ramakrishna, a Hindu devotee, who so impressed his hearers and pupils that many of them became ascetics after his death. Mozoomdar also looked upon this saint as his master, but Mozoomdar works for holiness in the world, in it but not of it, as Jesus taught.

Vivekananda's address before the parliament was broad as the heavens above us, embracing the best in all religions, as the ultimate universal religion — charity to all mankind, good works for the love of God, not for fear of punishment or hope of reward. He is a great favorite at the parliament, from the grandeur of his sentiments and his appearance as well. If he merely crosses the platform he is applauded, and this marked approval of thousands he accepts in a childlike spirit of gratification, without a trace of conceit. It must be a strange experience too for this humble young Brahmin monk, this sudden transition from poverty and self-effacement to affluence and aggrandizement. When asked if he knew anything of those brothers in the Himalayas so firmly believed in by the Theosophists, he answered with the simple statement, "I have never met one of them," as much as to imply, "There may be such persons, but though I am at home in the Himalayas, I have yet to come across them."

At The Parliament Of Religions

(The Dubuque, Iowa, *Times*, September 29, 1893)

WORLD'S FAIR, Sept. 28. — (Special.) — The Parliament of religions reached a point where sharp acerbities develop. The thin veil of courtesy was maintained, of course, but behind it was ill feeling. Rev. Joseph Cook criticised the Hindoos sharply and was more sharply criticised in turn. He said that to speak of a universe that was not created is almost unpardonable nonsense, and the Asiatics retorted that a universe which had a beginning is a self-evident absurdity. Bishop J. P. Newman, firing at long range from the banks of the Ohio, declared that the orientals have insulted all the Christians of the United States by their misrepresentations of the missionaries, and the orientals, with their provokingly calm and supercilious smile, replied that this was simply the bishop's ignorance.

Buddhist Philosophy

In response to the question direct, three learned Buddhists gave us in remarkably plain and beautiful language their bed-rock belief about God, man and matter.

[Following this is a summary of Dharmapala's paper on "The World's Debt to Buddha", which he prefaced, as we learn from another source, by singing a Singhalese song of benediction. The article then continues:]

His [Dharmapala's] peroration was as pretty a thing as a Chicago audience ever heard. Demosthenes never exceeded it.

CANTANKEROUS REMARKS

Swami Vivekananda, the Hindoo monk, was not so fortunate. He was out of humor, or soon became so, apparently. He wore an orange robe and a pale yellow turban and dashed at once into a savage attack on Christian nations in these words: "We who have come from the east have sat here day after day and have been told in a patronizing way that we ought to accept Christianity because Christian nations are the most prosperous. We look about us and we see England the most prosperous Christian nation in the world, with her foot on the neck of 250,000,000 Asiatics. We look back into history and see that the prosperity of Christian Europe began with Spain.

Spain's prosperity began with the invasion of Mexico. Christianity wins its prosperity by cutting the throats of its fellow men. At such a price the Hindoo will not have prosperity."

And so they went on, each succeeding speaker getting more cantankerous, as it were.

* * *

(*Outlook*, October 7, 1893)

. . . The subject of Christian work in India calls Vivekananda, in his brilliant priestly orange, to his feet. He criticises the work of Christian missions. It is evident that he has not tried to understand Christianity, but neither, as he claims, have its priests made any effort to understand *his* religion, with its ingrained faiths and raceprejudices of thousands of years' standing. They have simply come, in his view, to throw scorn on his most sacred beliefs, and to undermine the morals and spiritualist of the people he has been set to teach.

* * *

(*Critic*, October 7, 1893)

But the most impressive figures of the Parliament were the Buddhist priest, H. Dharmapala of Ceylon, and the Hindoo monk, Suami Vivekananda. "If theology and dogma stand in your way in search of truth," said the former incisively, "put them aside. Learn to think without prejudice, to love all beings for love's sake, to express your convictions fearlessly, to lead a life of purity, and the sunlight of truth will illuminate you." But eloquent as were many of the brief speeches at this meeting, whose triumphant enthusiasm rightly culminated in the superb rendering by the Apollo Club of the Hallelujah chorus, no one expressed so well the spirit of the Parliament, its limitations and its finest influence, as did the Hindoo monk. I copy his address in full, but I can only suggest its effect upon the audience, for he is an orator by divine right, and his strong intelligent face in its picturesque setting of yellow and orange was hardly less interesting than these earnest words and the rich, rhythmical utterance he gave them.... [After quoting the greater part of Swamiji's Final Address, the article continues:]

Perhaps the most tangible result of the congress was the feeling it aroused in regard to foreign missions. The impertinence of sending half-educated theological students to instruct the wise and erudite Orientals was never brought home to an English-speaking audience more forcibly. It is only in the spirit of tolerance and sympathy that we are at liberty to touch their faith, and the exhorters who possess these qualities are rare. It is necessary to realize that we have quite as much to learn from the Buddhists

as they from us, and that only through harmony can the highest influence
be exerted.

LUCY MONROE.

Chicago, 3 Oct., 1893.

* * *

[To a request of the New York World of October 1, 1893, for "a sentiment
or expression regarding the significance of the great meeting" from each
representative, Swamiji replied with a quotation from the Gita and one from
Vyâsa:]

"I am He that am in every religion — like the thread that passes
through a string of pearls." "Holy, perfect and pure men are seen in all
creeds, therefore they all lead to the same truth — for how can nectar be the
outcome of poison?"

Personal Traits

(*Critic*, October 7, 1893)

. . . It was an outgrowth of the Parliament of Religions, which opened our eyes to the fact that the philosophy of the ancient creeds contains much beauty for the moderns. When we had once clearly perceived this, our interest in their exponents quickened, and with characteristic eagerness we set out in pursuit of knowledge. The most available means of obtaining it, after the close of the Parliament, was through the addresses and lectures of Swami Vivekananda, who is still in this city [Chicago]. His original purpose in coming to this country was to interest Americans in the starting of new industries among the Hindoos, but he has abandoned this for the present, because he finds that, as "the Americans are the most charitable people in the world," every man with a purpose comes here for assistance in carrying it out. When asked about the relative condition of the poor here and in India, he replied that our poor would be princes there, and that he had been taken through the worst quarter of the city only to find it, from the standpoint of his knowledge, comfortable and even pleasant.

A Brahmin of the Brahmins, Vivekananda gave up his rank to join the brotherhood of monks, where all pride of caste is voluntarily relinquished. And yet he bears the mark of race upon his person. His culture, his eloquence, and his fascinating personality have given us a new idea of Hindoo civilization. He is an interesting figure, his fine, intelligent, mobile face in its setting of yellows, and his deep, musical voice prepossessing one at once in his favor. So it is not strange that he has been taken up by the literary clubs, has preached and lectured in churches, until the life of Buddha and the doctrines of his faith have grown familiar to us. He speaks without notes, presenting his facts and his conclusions with the greatest art, the most convincing sincerity; and rising at times to a rich, inspiring eloquence. As learned and cultivated, apparently, as the most accomplished Jesuit, he has also something Jesuitical in the character of his mind; but though the little sarcasms thrown into his discourses are as keen as a rapier, they are so delicate as to be lost on many tof his hearers. Nevertheless his courtesy is unfailing, for these thrusts are never pointed so directly at our customs as to be rude. At present he contents himself with enlightening us in regard to his religion and the words of its philosophers. He looks forward to the time when we shall pass beyond idolatry — now necessary in his opinion to the ignorant classes — beyond worship, even, to a knowledge of the presence of God in nature, of the divinity and responsibility of man. "Work out your own salvation," he says with the dying Buddha; "I cannot help you. No man can help you. Help yourself."

LUCY MONROE.

Reincarnation

(*Evanston Index*, October 7, 1893)

At the Congregational Church, during the past week, there have been given a course of lectures which in nature much resembled the Religious Parliament which has just been completed. The lecturers were Dr. Carl van Bergen of Sweden, and Suami Vivekananda, the Hindu monk. ... Suami Vivekananda is a representative from India to the Parliament of Religions. He has attracted a great deal of attention on account of his unique attire in Mandarin colors, by his magnetic presence and by his brilliant oratory and wonderful exposition of Hindu philosophy. His stay in Chicago has been a continual ovation. The course of lectures was arranged to cover three evenings.

[The lectures of Saturday and Tuesday evenings are listed without Comment; then the article continues:]

On Thursday evening Oct. 5, Dr. von Bergen spoke on "Huldine Beamish, the Founder of the King's Daughters of Sweden," and "Reincarnation" was the subject treated by the Hindu monk. The latter was very interesting; the views being those that are not often heard in this part of the world. The doctrine of reincarnation of the soul, while comparatively new and little understood in this country, is well-known in the east, being the foundation of nearly all the religions of those people. Those that do not use it as dogma, do not say anything against it. The main point to be decided in regard to the doctrine is, as to whether we have had a past. We know that we have a present and feel sure of a future. Yet how can there be a present without a past? Modern science has proved that matter exists and continues to exist. Creation is merely a change in appearance. We are not sprung out of nothing. Some regard God as the common cause of everything and judge this a sufficient reason for existence. But in everything we must consider the phenomena; whence and from what matter springs. The same arguments that prove there is a future prove that there is a past. It is necessary that there should be causes other than God's will. Heredity is not able to give sufficient cause. Some say that we are not conscious of a former existence.

Many cases have been found where there are distinct reminiscences of a past. And here lies the germ of the theory. Because the Hindu is kind to dumb animals many believe that we believe in the reincarnation of souls in lower orders. They are not able to conceive of kindness to dumb animals being other than the result of superstition. An ancient Hindu priest defines religion as anything that lifts one up. Brutality is driven out, humanity gives way to divinity. The theory of incarnation does not confine man to this small earth. His soul can go to other, higher earths where he will be a loftier being, possessing, instead of five senses, eight, and continuing in this way he will at length approach the acme of perfection, divinity, and will be allowed to drink deep of oblivion in the "Islands of the Blest".

Hindu Civilisation

[Although the lecture at Streator on October 9 was well attended, the *Streator Daily Free Press* of October 9 ran the following somewhat dreary review:]

The lecture of this celebrated Hindoo at the Opera House, Saturday night, was very interesting. By comparative philology, he sought to establish the long admitted relationship between the Aryan races and their descendants in the new world. He mildly defended the caste system of India which keeps three-fourths of the people in utter and humiliating subjection, and boasted that the India of today was the same India that had watched for centuries the meteoric nations of the world flash across the horizon and sink into oblivion. In common with the people, he loves the past. He lives not for self, but for God. In his country a premium is placed on beggary and tramps, though not so distinguished in his lecture. When the meal is prepared, they wait for some man to come along who is first served, then the animals, the servants, the man of the house and lastly the woman of the household. Boys are taken at 10 years of age and are kept by professors for a period of ten to twenty years, educated and sent forth to resume their former occupations or to engage in a life of endless wandering, preaching, and praying, taking along only that which is given them to eat and wear, but never touching money. Vivekananda is of the latter class. Men approaching old age withdraw from the world, and after a period of study and prayer, when they feel themselves sanctified, they also go forward spreading the gospel. He observed that leisure was necessary for intellectual development and scored Americans for not educating the Indians whom Columbus found in a state of savagery. In this he exhibited a lack of knowledge of conditions. His talk was lamentably short and much was left unsaid of seeming greater importance than much that was said.

(It is clear from the above report that the American Press, for one reason or another, did not always give Swamiji an enthusiastic reception.)

An Interesting Lecture

(Wisconsin State Journal, November 21, 1893)

The lecture at the Congregational Church [Madison] last night by the celebrated Hindoo monk, Vivekananda, was an extremely interesting one, and contained much of sound philosophy and good religion. Pagan though he be, Christianity may well follow many of his teachings. His creed is as wide as the universe, taking in all religions, and accepting truth wherever it may be found. Bigotry and superstition and idle ceremony, he declared, have no place in "the religions of India".

The Hindoo Religion

(*Minneapolis Star*, November 25, 1893)

"Brahminism" in all its subtle attraction, because of its embodiment of ancient and truthful principles, was the subject which held an audience in closest attention last evening at the First Unitarian Church [Minneapolis], while Swami Vive Kananda expounded the Hindoo faith. It was an audience which included thoughtful women and men, for the lecturer had been invited by the "Peripatetics," and among the friends who shared the privilege with them were ministers of varied denominations, as well as students and scholars. Vive Kananda is a Brahmin priest, and he occupied the platform in his native garb, with caftan on head, orange colored coat confined at the waist with a red sash, and red nether garments.

He presented his faith in all sincerity, speaking slowly and clearly, convincing his hearers by quietness of speech rather than by rapid action. His words were carefully weighed, and each carried its meaning direct. He offered the simplest truths of the Hindoo religion, and while he said nothing harsh about Christianity, he touched upon it in such a manner as to place the faith of Brahma before all. The all-pervading thought and leading principle of the Hindoo religion is the inherent divinity of the soul; the soul is perfect, and religion is the manifestation of divinity already existing in man. The present is merely a line of demarkation between the past and future, and of the two tendencies in man, if the good preponderates he will move to a higher sphere, if the evil has power, he degenerates. These two are continually at work within him; what elevates him is virtue, that which degenerates is evil.

Kananda will speak at the First Unitarian Church tomorrow morning.

* * *

(*Des Moines News*, November 28, 1893)

Swami Vivekananda, the talented scholar from the far-off India, spoke at the Central church last night [November 27]. He was a representative of his country and creed at the recent parliament of religions assembled in Chicago during the world's fair. Rev. H. O. Breeden introduced the speaker to the audience. He arose and after bowing to his audience, commenced his lecture, the subject of which was "Hindoo Religion". His lecture was not confined to any line of thought but consisted more of some of his own philosophical views relative to his religion and others. He holds that one must embrace all the religions to become the perfect Christian. What is not found in one religion is supplied by another. They are all right and necessary for the true Christian. When you send a missionary to our country he becomes a Hindoo Christian and I a Christian Hindoo. I have often been asked in this country if I am going to try to convert the people here. I take this for an insult. I do not believe in this idea of conversion. To-day we have a sinful man; tomorrow according to your idea he is converted and by and by attains unto holiness. Whence comes this change? How do you explain it? The man has not a new soul for the soul must die. You say he is changed by God. God is perfect, all powerful and is purity itself. Then after this man is converted he is that same God minus the purity he gave that man to become holy. There is in our country two words which have an altogether different meaning than they do in this country. They are "religion" and "sect". We hold that religion embraces all religions. We tolerate everything but intoleration. Then there is that word "sect". Here it embraces those sweet people who wrap themselves up in their mantle of charity and say, "We are right; you are wrong." It reminds me of the story of the two frogs. A frog was born in a well and lived its whole life in that well. One day a frog from the sea fell in that well and they commenced to talk about the sea. The frog whose home was in the well asked the visitor how large the sea was, but was unable to get an intelligent answer. Then the at home frog jumped from one corner of the well to another and asked his visitor if the sea was that large. He said yes. The frog jumped again and said, "Is the sea that large?" and receiving an affirmative reply, he said to himself, "This frog must be a liar; I will put him out of my well." That is the way with these sects. They seek to eject and trample those who do not believe as they do.

The Hindoo Monk

(*Appeal-Avalanche*, January 16, 1894)

Swami Vive Kananda, the Hindoo monk, who is to lecture at the Auditorium [Memphis] tonight, is one of the most eloquent men who has ever appeared on the religious or lecture platform in this country. His matchless oratory, deep penetration into things occult, his cleverness in debate, and great earnestness captured the closest attention of the world's thinking men at the World's Fair Parliament of Religion, and the admiration of thousands of people who have since heard him during his lecture tour through many of the states of the Union.

In conversation he is a most pleasant gentleman; his choice of words are the gems of the English language, and his general bearing ranks him with the most cultured people of Western etiquette and custom. As a companion he is a most charming man, and as a conversationalist he is, perhaps, not surpassed in the drawing-rooms of any city in the Western World. He speaks English not only distinctly, but fluently, and his ideas, as new as sparkling, drop from his tongue in a perfectly bewildering overflow of ornamental language.

Swami Vive Kananda, by his inherited religion or early teachings, grew up a Brahmin, but becoming converted to the Hindoo religion he sacrificed his rank and became a Hindoo priest, or as known in the country of oriental ideality, a sanyasin. He had always been a close student of the wonderful and mysterious works of nature as drawn from God's high conception, and with years spent as both a student and teacher in the higher colleges of that eastern country, he acquired a knowledge that has given him a worldwide reputation as one of the most thoughtful scholars of the age.

His wonderful first address before the members of the World's Fair Parliament stamped him at once as a leader in that great body of religious thinkers. During the session he was frequently heard in defence of his religion, and some of the most beautiful and philosophical gems that grace the English language rolled from his lips there in picturing the higher duties that man owed to man and to his Creator. He is an artist in thought, an idealist in belief and a dramatist on the platform.

Since his arrival in Memphis he has been guest of Mr. Hu L. Brinkley, where he has received calls day and evening from many in Memphis who desired to pay their respects to him. He is also an informal guest at the Tennessee Club and was a guest at the reception given by Mrs. S. R. Shepherd, Saturday evening. Col. R. B. Snowden gave a dinner at his home at Annesdale in honor of the distinguished visitor on Sunday, where he met Assistant Bishop Thomas F. Gailor, Rev. Dr. George Patterson and a number of other clergymen.

Yesterday afternoon he lectured before a large and fashionable audience composed of the members of the Nineteenth Century Club in the rooms of the club in the Randolph Building. Tonight he will be heard at the Auditorium on "Hindooism".

Plea For Tolerance

(*Memphis Commercial*, January 17, 1894)

An audience of fair proportions gathered last night at the Auditorium to greet the celebrated Hindu monk. Swami Vive Kananda, in his lecture on Hinduism.

He was introduced in a brief but informing address by Judge R. J. Morgan, who gave a sketch of the development of the great Aryan race, from which development have come the Europeans and the Hindus alike, so tracing a racial kinship between the people of America and the speaker who was to address them.

The eminent Oriental was received with liberal applause, and heard with attentive interest throughout. He is a man of fine physical presence, with regular bronze features and form of fine proportions. He wore a robe of pink silk, fastened at the waist with a black sash, black trousers and about his head was gracefully draped a turban of yellow India silk. His delivery is very good, his use of English being perfect as regards choice of words and correctness of grammar and construction. The only inaccuracy of pronunciation is in the accenting of words at times upon a wrong syllable. Attentive listeners, however, probably lost few words, and their attention was well rewarded by an address full of original thought, information and broad wisdom. The address might fitly be called a plea for universal tolerance, illustrated by remarks concerning the religion of India. This spirit, he contended, the spirit of tolerance and love, is the central inspiration of all religions which are worthy, and this, he thinks, is the end to be secured by any form of faith.

His talk concerning Hinduism was not strictly circumstantial. His attempt was rather to give an analysis of its spirit than a story of its legends or a picture of its forms. He dwelt upon only a few of the distinctive credal or ritual features of his faith, but these he explained most clearly and perspicuously. He gave a vivid account of the mystical features of Hinduism, out of which the so often misinterpreted theory of reincarnation has grown. He explained how his religion ignored the differentiations of time, how, just as all men believe in the present and the future of the soul, so the faith of Brahma believes in its past. He made it clear, too, how his faith does not believe in "original sin," but bases all effort and aspiration on the belief of the perfectibility of humanity. Improvement and purification, he contends, must be based upon hope. The development of man is a return to an original perfection. This perfection must come through the practice of holiness and love. Here he showed how his own people have practiced these qualities, how India has been a land of refuge for the oppressed, citing the instance of the welcome given by the Hindus to the Jews when Titus sacked Jerusalem and destroyed the Temple

In a graphic way he told that the Hindus do not lay much stress upon forms. Sometimes every member of the family will differ in their adherence to sects, but all will worship God by worshipping the spirit of love which is His central attribute. The Hindus, he says, hold that there is good in all religions, that all religions are embodiments of man's inspiration for holiness, and being such, all should be respected. He illustrated this by a citation from the Vedas [?], in which varied religions are symbolized as the differently formed vessels with which different men came to bring water from a spring. The forms of the vessels are many, but the water of truth is what all seek to fill their vessels with. God knows all forms of faith, he thinks, and will recognize his own name no matter what it is called, or what may be the fashion of the homage paid him.

The Hindus, he continued, worship the same God as the Christians. The Hindu trinity of Brahma, Vishnu, Siva is merely an embodiment of God the creator, the preserver and the destroyer. That the three are considered three instead of one is simply a corruption due to the fact that general humanity must have its ethics made tangible. So likewise the material images of Hindu gods are simply symbols of divine qualities.

He told, in explanation of the Hindu doctrine of incarnation, the story of Krishna, who was born by immaculate conception and the story of whom greatly resembles the story of Jesus. The teaching of Krishna, he claims, is the doctrine of love for its own sake, and he expressed [it] by the words "If the fear of the Lord is the beginning of religion, the love of God is its end."

His entire lecture cannot be sketched here, but it was a masterly appeal for brotherly love, and an eloquent defense of a beautiful faith. The conclusion was especially fine, when he acknowledged his readiness to accept Christ but must also bow to Krishna and to Buddha; and when, with a fine picture of the cruelty of civilization, he refused to hold Christ responsible for the crimes of progress.

Manners And Customs In India

(*Appeal-Avalanche*, January 21, 1894)

Swami Vive Kananda, the Hindoo monk, delivered a lecture at La Salette Academy [Memphis] yesterday afternoon. Owing to the pouring rain, a very small audience was present.

The subject discussed was "Manners and Customs in India." Vive Kananda is advancing theories of religious thought which find ready lodgment in the minds of some of the most advanced thinkers of this as well as other cities of America.

His theory is fatal to the orthodox belief, as taught by the Christian teachers. It has been the supreme effort of Christian America to enlighten the beclouded minds of heathen India, but it seems that the oriental splendor of Kananda's religion has eclipsed the beauty of the old-time Christianity, as taught by our parents, and will find a rich field in which to thrive in the minds of some of the better educated of America.

This is a day of "fads," and Kananda seems to be filling a "long felt want." He is, perhaps, one of the most learned men of his country, and possesses a wonderful amount of personal magnetism, and his hearers are charmed by his eloquence. While he is liberal in his views, he sees very little to admire in the orthodox Christianity. Kananda has received more marked attention in Memphis than almost any lecturer or minister that has ever visited the city.

If a missionary to India was as cordially received as the Hindoo monk is here the work of spreading the gospel of Christ in heathen lands would be well advanced. His lecture yesterday afternoon was an interesting one from a historic point of view. He is thoroughly familiar with the history and traditions of his native country, from very ancient history up to the present, and can describe the various places and objects of interest there with grace and ease.

During his lecture he was frequently interrupted by questions propounded by the ladies in the audience, and he answered all queries without the least hesitancy, except when one of the ladies asked a question with the purpose of drawing him out into a religious discussion. He refused to be led from the original subject of his discourse and informed the interrogator that at another time he would give his views on the "transmigration of the soul," etc.

In the course of his remarks he said that his grandfather was married when he was 3 years old and his father married at 18, but he had never married at all. A monk is not forbidden to marry, but if he takes a wife she becomes a monk with the same powers and privileges and occupies the same social position as her husband.

In answer to a question, he said there were no divorces in India for any cause, but if, after 14 years of married life, there were no children in the family, the husband was allowed to marry another with the wife's consent, but if she objected he could not marry again. His description of the ancient mausoleums and temples were beautiful beyond comparison, and goes to show that the ancients possessed scientific knowledge far superior to the most expert artisans of the present day.

Swami Vivi Kananda will appear at the Y. M. H. A. Hall to-night for the last time in this city. He is under contract with the "Slayton Lyceum Bureau," of Chicago, to fill a three-years' engagement in this country. He will leave tomorrow for Chicago, where he has an engagement for the night of the 25th.

(Detroit Tribune, February 15, 1894)

Last evening a good sized audience had the privilege of seeing and listening to the famous Hindu Monk of the Brahmo Samaj, Swami Vive Kananda, as he lectured at the Unitarian Church under the auspices of the Unity Club. He appeared in native costume and made with his handsome face and stalwart figure a distinguished appearance. His eloquence held the audience in rapt attention and brought out applause at frequent intervals. He spoke of the "Manners and Customs of India" and presented the subject in the most perfect English. He said they did not call their country India nor themselves Hindus. Hindostan was the name of the country and they were Brahmans. In ancient times they spoke Sanscrit. In that language the reason and meaning of a word was explained and made quite evident but now that is all gone. Jupiter in Sanscrit meant "Father in Heaven." All the languages of northern India were now practically the same, but if he should go into the southern part of that country he could not converse with the people. In the words father, mother, sister, brother, etc.; the Sanscrit gave very similar pronunciations. This and other facts lead him to think we all come from the common stock, Aryans. Nearly all branches of this race have lost their identity

There were four castes, the priests, the landlords and military people, the trades people and the artisans, laborers and servants. In the first three castes the boys as the ages of ten, eleven and thirteen respectively are placed in the hands of professors of universities and remain with them until thirty, twenty-five and twenty years old, respectively. ... In ancient times both boys and girls were instructed, but now only the boys are favored. An effort, however, is being made to rectify the long-existing wrong. A good share of the philosophy and laws of the land is the work of women during the ancient times, before barbarians started to rule the land. In the eyes of the Hindu the woman now has her rights. She holds her own and has the law on her side.

When the student returns from college he is allowed to marry and have a household. Husband and wife must bear the work and both have their rights. In the military caste the daughters oftentimes can choose their husbands, but in all other cases all arrangements are made by the parents. There is a constant effort now being made to remedy infant marriage. The marriage ceremony is very beautiful, each touches the heart of the other and they swear before God and the assemblage that they will prove faithful to each other. No man can be a priest until he marries. When a man attends public worship he is always attended by his wife. In his worship the Hindu performs five ceremonies, worship of his God, of his forefathers, of the poor, of the dumb animals, and of learning. As long as a Hindu has anything in the house a guest must never want. When he is satisfied then the children, then father and mother partake. They are the poorest nation in the world, yet except in times of famine no one dies of hunger. Civilization is a great work. But in comparison the statement is made that in England one in every 400 is a drunkard, while in India the proportion is one to every million. A description was given of the ceremony of burning the dead. No publicity is made except in the case of some great nobleman. After a fifteen days' fast gifts are given by the relatives in behalf of the forefathers to the poor or for the formation of some institution. On moral matters they stand head and shoulders above all other nations.

Hindoo Philosophy

(*Detroit Free Press*, February 16, 1894)

The second lecture of the Hindoo monk, Swami Vive Kananda, was given last evening at the Unitarian church to a large and very appreciative audience. The expectation of the audience that the speaker would enlighten them regarding "Hindoo Philosophy," as the lecture was entitled, was gratified to only a limited extent. Allusions were made to the philosophy of Buddha, and the speaker was applauded when he said that Buddhism was the first missionary religion of the world, and that it had secured the largest number of converts without the shedding of a drop of blood; but he did not tell his audience anything about the religion or philosophy of Buddha. He made a number of cute little jabs at the Christian religion, and alluded to the trouble and misery that had been caused by its introduction into heathen countries, but he skilfully avoided any comparison between the social condition of the people in his own land and that of the people to whom he was speaking. In a general way he said the Hindoo philosophers taught from a lower truth to a higher; whereas, a person accepting a newer Christian doctrine is asked and expected to throw his former belief all away and accept the newer in its entirety. "It is an idle dream when all of us will have the same religious views," said he. "No emotion can be produced except by clashing elements acting upon the mind. It is the revulsion of change, the new light, the presentation of the new to the old, that elicits sensation."

[As the first lecture had antagonised some people, the *Free Press* reporter was very cautious. Fortunately, however, the Detroit Tribune consistently upheld Swamiji, and thus in its report of February 16 we get some idea of his lecture on "Hindu Philosophy," although the *Tribune* reporter seems to have taken somewhat sketchy notes:]

(*Detroit Tribune*, February 16, 1894)

The Brahman monk, Swami Vive Kananda, again lectured last evening at the Unitarian church, his topic being "Hindu Philosophy." The speaker dealt for a time with general philosophy and metaphysics, but said that he would devote the lecture to that part pertaining to religion. There is a sect that believes in a soul, but are agnostic in relation to God. Buddahism [sic] was a great moral religion, but they could not live long without believing in a god. Another sect known as the giants [Jains] believe in the soul, but not in the moral government of the country. There were several millions of this sect in India. Their priests and monks tie a handkerchief over their faces believing if their hot breath comes in contact with man or beast death will ensue.

Among the orthodox, all believe in the revelation. Some think every cord in the Bible comes directly from God. The stretching of the meaning of a word would perhaps do in most religions, but in that of the Hindus they have the Sanscrit, which always retains the full meaning and reasons of the world.

The distinguished Oriental thought there was a sixth sense far greater than any of the five we know we possess. It was the truth of revelation. A man may read all the books on religion in the world and yet be the greatest blackguard in the country. Revelation means later reports of spiritual discoveries.

The second position some take is a creation without beginning or end. Suppose there was a time when the world did not exist; what was God doing then? To the Hindus the creation was only one of forms. One man is born with a healthy body, is of good family and grows up a godly man. Another is born with a maimed and crooked body and develops into a wicked man and pays the penalty. Why must a just and holy god create one with so many advantages and the other with disadvantages? The person has no choice. The evildoer has a consciousness of his guilt. The difference between virtue and vice was expounded. If God willed all things there would be an end to all science. How far can man go down? Is it possible for man to go back to brute again?

Kananda was glad he was a Hindu. When Jerusalem was destroyed by the Romans several thousand [Jews] settled in India. When the Persians were driven from their country by the Arabs several thousand found refuge in the same country and none were molested. The Hindu, believe all religions are true, but theirs antedates all others. Missionaries are never molested by the Hindus. The first English missionaries mere prevented from landing in that country by English and it was a Hindu that interceded for them and gave them the first hand. Religion is that which believes in all. Religion was compared to the blind men and the elephant. Each man felt of a special part and from it drew his conclusions of what an elephant was. Each was right in his way and yet all were needed to form a whole. Hindu philosophers say "truth to truth, lower truth to higher." It is an idle dream of those who think that all will at some time think alike, for that would be the death of religion. Every religion breaks up into little sects, each claiming to he the true one and all the others wrong. Persecution is unknown in Buddahism. They sent out the first missionaries and are the only ones who can say they have converted millions without the shedding of a single drop of blood. Hindus, with all their faults and superstitions, never persecute. The speaker wanted to know how it was the Christians allowed such iniquities as are everywhere present in Christian countries.

Miracles

(*Evening News*, February 17, 1894)

I cannot comply with the request of The News to work a miracle in proof of my religion," said Vive Kananda to a representative of this paper, after being shown The News editorial on the subject. "In the first place, I am no miracle worker, and in the second place the pure Hindoo religion I profess is not based on miracles. We do not recognize such a thing as miracles. There are wonders wrought beyond our five senses, but they are operated by some law. Our religion has nothing to do with them. Most of the strange things which are done in India and reported in the foreign papers are sleight-of-hand tricks or hypnotic illusions. They are not the performances of the wise men. These do not go about the country performing their wonders in the market places for pay. They can be seen and known only by those who seek to know the truth, and not moved by childish curiosity."

The Divinity Of Man

(*Detroit Free Press*, February 18, 1894)

Swami Vive Kananda, Hindoo philosopher and priest, concluded his series of lectures, or rather, sermons, at the Unitarian church last night, speaking on "The Divinity of God" [sic]. (Actually the subject was "The Divinity of Man".) In spite of the bad weather, the church was crowded almost to the doors half an hour before the eastern brother — as he likes to be called — appeared. All professions and business occupations were represented in the attentive audience — lawyers, judges, ministers of the gospel, merchants, rabbi — not to speak of the many ladies who have by their repeated attendance and rapt attention shown a decided inclination to shower adulation upon the dusky visitor whose drawing-room attraction is as great as his ability in the rostrum.

The lecture last night was less descriptive than preceding ones, and for nearly two hours Vive Kananda wove a metaphysical texture on affairs human and divine so logical that he made science appear like common sense. It was a beautiful logical garment that he wove, replete with as many bright colors and as attractive and pleasing to contemplate as one of the many-hued fabrics made by hand in his native land and scented with the most seductive fragrance of the Orient. This dusky gentleman uses poetical imagery as an artist uses colors, and the hues are laid on just where they belong, the result being somewhat bizarre in effect, and yet having a peculiar fascination. Kaleidoscopic were the swiftly succeeding logical conclusions, and the deft manipulator was rewarded for his efforts from time to time by enthusiastic applause.

The lecture was prefaced with the statement that the speaker had been asked many questions. A number of these he preferred to answer privately, but three he had selected, for reasons which would appear, to answer from the pulpit. They were: (This and the next four paragraphs appear in Vol. IV of the Complete Works under the heading, "Is India a Benighted Country?")

"Do the people of India throw their children into the laws of the crocodiles?"

"Do they kill themselves beneath the wheels of the juggernaut?"

"Do they burn widows with their husbands?"

The first question the lecturer treated in the vein that an American abroad would answer inquiries about Indians running around in the streets of New York and similar myths which are even to-day entertained by many persons on the continent. The statement was too ludicrous to give a serious response to it. When asked by certain well-meaning but ignorant people why they gave only female children to the crocodiles, he could only ironically reply that probably it was because they were softer and more tender and could be more easily masticated by the inhabitants of the rivers in the benighted country. Regarding the juggernaut legend the lecturer explained the old practice in the sacred city and remarked that possibly a few in their zeal to grasp the rope and participate in the drawing of the car slipped and fell and were so destroyed. Some such mishaps had been exaggerated into the distorted version from which the good people of other countries shrank with horror. Vive Kananda denied that the people burned widows. It was true, however, that widows had burned themselves. In the few cases where this had happened, they had been urged not to do so by the priests and holy men who were always opposed to suicide Where the devoted widows insisted, stating that they desired to accompany their husbands in the transformation that had taken place they were obliged to submit to the fiery test. That is, they thrust their hands within the flames and if they permitted them to be consumed no further opposition was placed in the way of the fulfilment of their desires. But India is not the only country where women who have loved have followed immediately the loved one through the realms of immortality; suicide in such cases have occurred in every land. It is an uncommon bit of fanaticism in any country; as unusual in India as elsewhere. No, the speaker repeated, the people do not burn women in India; nor have they ever burned witches.

Proceeding to the lecture proper, Vive Kananda proceeded to analyze the physical, mental and soul attributes of life. The body is but a shell; the mind something that acts but a brief and fantastic part; while the soul has distinct individuality in itself. To realize the infinity of self is to attain "freedom" which is the Hindoo word for "salvation." By a convincing manner of argument the lecturer showed that every soul is something independent, for if it were dependent, it could not acquire immortality. He related a story from the old legends of his country to illustrate the manner in which the realization of this may come to the individual. A lioness leaping towards a sheep in the act gave birth to a cub. The lioness died and the cub was given suck by the sheep and for many years thought itself a sheep and acted like one. But one day another lion appeared and led the first lion to a lake where he looked in and saw his resemblance to the other lion. At that he roared and realized else full majesty of self. Many people are like the lion masquerading as a sheep and get into a corner, call themselves sinners and demean themselves in every imaginable fashion, not yet seeing the perfection and divinity which lies in self. The ego of man and woman is the soul. If the soul is independent, how then can it be isolated from the infinite whole? Just as the great sun shines on a lake and numberless reflections are the result, so the soul is distinct like each reflection, although the great source is recognized and appreciated. The soul is sexless. When it has realized the condition of absolute freedom, what could it have to do with sex which is physical? In this connection the lecturer delved deeply into the water of Swedenborgian philosophy, or religion, and the connection between the conviction of the Hindoo and the spiritual expressions of faith on the part of the more modern holy man was fully apparent. Swedenborg seemed like a European successor of an early Hindoo priest, clothing in modern garb an ancient conviction; a line of thought that the greatest of French philosophers and novelists [Balzac?] saw fit to embody in his elevating tale of the perfect soul. Every individual has in himself perfection. It lies within the dark recesses of his physical being. To say that a man has become good because God gave him a portion of His perfection is to conceive the Divine Being as God minus just so much perfection as he has imparted to a person on this earth. The inexorable law of science proves that the soul is individual and must have perfection within itself, the attainment of which means freedom, not salvation, and the realization of individual infinity. Nature! God! Religion! It is all one.

The religions are all good. A bubble of air in a glass of water strives to join with the mass of air without; in oil, vinegar and other materials of differing density its efforts are less or more retarded according to the liquid. So the soul struggles through various mediums for the attainment of its individual infinity. One religion is best adapted to a certain people because of habits of life, association, hereditary traits and climatic influences. Another religion is suited to another people for similar reasons. All that is, is best seemed to be the substance of the lecturer's conclusions. To try abruptly to change a nation's religion would be like a man who sees a river flowing from the Alps. He criticizes the way it has taken. Another man views the mighty stream descending from the Himalayas, a stream that has been running for generations and thousands of years, and says that it has not taken the shortest and best route. The Christian pictures God as a personal being seated somewhere above us. The Christian cannot necessarily be happy in Heaven unless he can stand on the edge of the golden streets and from time to time gaze down into the other place and see the difference. Instead of the golden rule, the Hindoo believes in the doctrine that all non-self is good and all self is bad, and through this belief the attainment of the individual infinity and the freedom of the soul at the proper time will be fulfilled. How excessively vulgar, stated Vive Kananda, was the golden rule! Always self! always self! was the Christian creed. To do unto others as you would be done by! It was a horrible, barbarous, savage creed, but he did not desire to decry the Christian creed, for those who are satisfied with it to them it is well adapted. Let the great stream flow on, and he is a fool who would try to change its course, when nature will work out the solution. Spiritualist (in the true acceptance of the word) and fatalist, Vive Kananda emphasized his opinion that all was well and he had no desire to convert Christians. They were Christians; it was well. He was a Hindoo; that, also, was well. In his country different creeds were formulated for the needs of people of different grades of intelligence, all this marking the progress of spiritual evolution. The Hindoo religion was not one of self; ever egotistical in its aspirations, ever holding up promises of reward or threats of punishment. It shows to the individual he may attain infinity by non-self. This system of bribing men to become Christians, alleged to have come from God, who manifested Himself to certain men on earth, is atrocious. It is horribly demoralizing and the Christian creed, accepted literally, has a shameful effect upon the moral natures of the bigots who accept it, retarding the time when the infinity of self may be attained.

* * *

[The Tribune reporter, perhaps the same who had earlier heard "giants" for "Jains," this time heard "bury" for "burn"; but otherwise, with the exception of Swamiji's statements regarding the golden rule, he seems to have reported more or less accurately:]

(Detroit Tribune, February 18, 1894)

Swami Vive Kananda at the Unitarian Church last night declared that widows were never buried [burned] alive in India through religion or law, but the act in all cases had been voluntary on the part of the women. The practice had been forbidden by one emperor, but it had gradually grown again until a stop was put to it by the English government. Fanatics existed in all religions, the Christian as well as the Hindu. Fanatics in India had been known to hold their hands over their heads in penance for so long a time that the arm had gradually grown stiff in that position, and so remained ever after. So, too, men had made a vow to stand still in one position. These persons would in time lose all control of the lower limbs and never after be able to walk. All religions were true, and the people practiced morality, not because of any divine command, but because of its own good. Hindus, he said, did not believe in conversion, calling it perversion. Associations, surroundings and educations were responsible for the great number of religions, and how foolish it was for an exponent of one religion to declare that another man's belief was wrong. It was as reasonable as a man from Asia coming to America and after viewing the course of the Mississippi to say to it: "You are running entirely wrong. You will have to go back to the starting place and commence it all over again." It would be just as foolish for a man in America to visit the Alps and after following the course of a river to the German Sea to inform it that its course was too tortuous and that the only remedy would be to flow as directed. The golden rule, he declared, was as old as the earth itself and to it could be traced all rules of morality [sic]. Man is a bundle of selfishness. He thought the hell fire theory was all nonsense. There could not be perfect happiness when it was known that suffering existed. He ridiculed the manner some religious persons have while praying. The Hindu, he said, closed his eyes and communed with the inner spirit, while some Christians he had seen had seemed to stare at some point as if they saw God seated upon his heavenly throne. In the matter of religion there were two extremes, the bigot and the atheist. There was some good in the atheist, but the bigot lived only for his own little self. He thanked some anonymous person who had sent him a picture of the heart of Jesus. This he thought a manifestation of bigotry. Bigots belong to no religion. They are a singular phenomena [sic].

The Love Of God

(The *Detroit Free Press* report of this lecture is printed in Vol. VIII of the Complete Works.)

(*Detroit Tribune*, February 21, 1894)

The First Unitarian Church was crowded last night to hear Vive Kananda. The audience was composed of people who came from Jefferson Avenue and the upper part of Woodward Avenue. Most of it was ladies who seemed deeply interested in the address and applauded several remarks of the Brahman with much enthusiasm.

The love that was dwelt upon by the speaker was not the love that goes with passion, but a pure and holy love that one in India feels for his God. As Vive Kananda stated at the commencement of his address the subject was "The Love the Indian Feels for His God." But he did not preach to his text. The major portion of his address was an attack on the Christian religion. The religion of the Indian and the love of his God was the minor portion. The points in his address were illustrated with several applicable anecdotes of famous people in the history. The subjects of the anecdotes were renowned Mogul emperors of his native land and not of the native Hindu kings.

The professors of religion were divided into two classes by the lecturer, the followers of knowledge and the followers of devotion. The end in the life of the followers of knowledge was experience. The end in the life of the devotee was love.

Love, he said, was a sacrifice. It never takes, but it always gives. The Hindu never asks anything of his God, never prayed for salvation and a happy hereafter, but instead lets his whole soul go out to his God in an entrancing love. That beautiful state of existence could only be gained when a person felt an overwhelming want of God. Then God came in all of His fullness.

There were three different ways of looking at God. One was to look upon Him as a mighty personage and fall down and worship His might. Another was to worship Him as a father. In India the father always punished the children and an element of fear was mixed with the regard and love for a father. Still another way to think of God was as a mother. In India a mother was always truly loved and reverenced. That was the Indian's way of looking at their God.

Kananda said that a true lover of God would be so wrapt up in his love that he would have no time to stop and tell members of another sect that they were following the wrong road to secure the God, and strive to bring him to his way of thinking.

* * *

(Detroit Journal)

If Vive Kananda, the Brahmin monk, who is delivering a lecture course in this city could be induced to remain for a week longer, the largest hall in Detroit would not hold the crowds which would be anxious to hear him. He has become a veritable fad, as last evening every seat in the Unitarian church was occupied, and many were compelled to stand throughout the entire lecture.

The speaker's subject was, "The Love of God". His definition of love was "something absolutely unselfish; that which has no thought beyond the glorification and adoration of the object upon which our affections are bestowed." Love, he said, is a quality which bows down And worships and asks nothing in return. Love of God, he thought, was different. God is not accepted, he said, because we really need him, except for selfish purposes. His lecture was replete with story and anecdote, all going to show the selfish motive underlying the motive of love for God. The Songs of Solomon were cited by the lecturer as the most beautiful portion of the Christian Bible and yet he had heard with deep regret that there was a possibility of their being removed. "In fact," he declared, as a sort clinching argument at the close, "the love of God appears to be based upon a theory of 'What can I get out of it?' Christians are so selfish in their love that they are continually asking God to give them something, including all manner of selfish things. Modern religion is, therefore, nothing but a mere hobby and fashion and people flock to church like a lot of sheep."

The Women Of India

(*Detroit Free Press*, March 25, 1894)

Kananda lectured last night at the Unitarian church on "The Women of India." The speaker reverted to the women of ancient India, showing in what high regard they are held in the holy books, where women were prophetesses. Their spirituality then was admirable. It is unfair to judge women in the east by the western standard. In the west woman is the wife; in the east she is the mother. The Hindoos worship the idea of mother, and even the monks are required to touch the earth with their foreheads before their mothers. Chastity is much esteemed.

The lecture was one of the most interesting Kananda has delivered and he was warmly received.

* * *

(Detroit Evening News, March 25, 1894)

Swami Vive Kananda lectured at the Unitarian Church last night on "The Women of India, Past, Medieval and the Present." He stated that in India the woman was the visible manifestation of God and that her whole life was given up to the thought that she was a mother, and to be a perfect mother she must be chaste. No mother in India ever abandoned her offspring, he said, and defied any one to prove the contrary. The girls of India would die if they, like American girls, were obliged to expose half their bodies to the vulgar gaze of young men. He desired that India be judged from the standard of that country and not from this.

* * *

(*Tribune*, April 1, 1894)

While Swami Kananda was in Detroit he had a number of conversations, in which he answered questions regarding the women of India. It was the information he thus imparted that suggested a public lecture from him on this subject. But as he speaks without notes, some of the points he made in private conversation did not appear in his public address. Then his friends were in a measure disappointed. But one of his lady listeners has put on paper some of the things he told in his afternoon talks, and it is now for the first time given to the press:

To the great tablelands of the high Himalaya mountains first came the Aryans, and there to this day abides the pure type of Brahman, a people which we westerners can but dream of. Pure in thought, deed and action, so honest that a bag of gold left in a public place would be found unharmed twenty years after; so beautiful that, to use Kananda's own phrase, "to see a girl in the fields is to pause and marvel that God could make anything so exquisite." Their features are regular, their eyes and hair dark, and their skin the color which would be produced by the drops which fell from a pricked finger into a glass of milk. These are the Hindus in their pure type, untainted and untrammeled.

As to their property laws, the wife's dowry belongs to her exclusively, never becoming the property of the husband. She can sell or give away without his consent. The gifts from any one to herself, including those of the husband, are hers alone, to do with as she pleases.

Woman walks abroad without fear; she is as free as perfect trust in those about her can render her. There is no zenana in the Himalayas, and there is a part of India which the missionaries never reach. These villages are most difficult of access. These people, untouched by Mahometan influence, can but be reached by wearisome and toilsome climbing, and are unknown to Mahometan and Christian alike.

INDIA'S FIRST INHABITANTS

In the forest of India are found races of wild people — very wild, even to cannibalism. These are the original Indians and never were Aryan or Hindu.

As the Hindus settled in the country proper and spread over its vast area, corruptions of many kinds found home among them. The sun was scorching and the men exposed to it were dark in color.

Five generations are but needed to change the transparent glow of the white complexion of the dwellers of the Himalaya Mountains to the bronzed hue of the Hindu of India.

Kananda has one brother very fair and one darker than himself. His father and mother are fair. The women are apt to be, the cruel etiquette of the Zenana established for protection from the Mohammedans keeping them within doors, fairer. Kananda is thirty-one years old.

A CLIP AT AMERICAN MEN

Kananda asserts with an amused twinkle in his eye that American men amuse him. They profess to worship woman, but in his opinion they simply worship youth and beauty. They never fall in love with wrinkles and gray hair. In fact he is under a strong impression that American men once had a trick — inherited, to be sure — of burning up their old women. Modern history calls this the burning of witches. It was men who accused and condemned witches, and it was usually the old age of the victim that led her to the stake. So it is seen that burning women alive is not exclusively a Hindu custom. He thought that if it were remembered that the Christian church burned old women at the stake, there would be less horror expressed regarding the burning of Hindu widows.

BURNINGS COMPARED

The Hindu widow went to her death agony amid feasting and song, arrayed in her costliest garments and believing for the most part that such an act meant the glories of Paradise for herself and family. She was worshipped as a martyr and her name was enshrined among the family records.

However horrible the rite appears to us, it is a bright picture compared to the burning of the Christian witch who, considered a guilty thing from the first, was thrown in a stifling dungeon, tortured cruelly to extort confession, subjected to an infamous trial, dragged amid jeering to the stake and consoled amid her sufferings by the bystander's comfort that the burning of her body was but the symbol for hell's everlasting fires, in which her soul would suffer even greater torment.

MOTHERS ARE SACRED

Kananda says the Hindu is taught to worship the principle of motherhood. The mother outranks the wife. The mother is holy. The motherhood of God is more in his mind than the fatherhood.

All women, whatever the caste, are exempt from corporal punishment. Should a woman murder, her head is spared. She may be placed astride a donkey facing his tail. Thus riding through the streets a drummer shouts her crime, after which she is free, her humiliation being deemed sufficient punishment to serve as a preventive for further crime.

Should she care to repent, there are religious houses open to her, where she can become purified or she can at her own option at once enter the class of monks and so become a holy woman.

The question was put to Mr. Kananda whether the freedom thus allowed in the joining the monks without a superior over them did not tend to hypocrisy among the order, as he claims, of the purest of Hindu philosophers. Kananda assented, but explained that there is no one between the people and the monk. The monk has broken down all caste. A Brahmin will not touch the low-caste Hindu but let him or her become a monk and the mightiest will prostrate himself before the low-caste monk.

The people are obliged to take care of the monk, but only as long as they believe in his sincerity. Once condemned for hypocrisy he is called a liar and falls to the depths of mendicancy — a mere wandering beggar — inspiring no respect.

OTHER THOUGHTS

A woman has the right of way with even a prince. When the studious Greeks visited Hindustan to learn of the Hindu, all doors were open to them, but when the Mohammedan with his sword and the Englishman with his bullets came their doors were closed. Such guests were not welcomed. As Kananda deliciously words it: "When the tiger comes we close our doors until he has passed by."

The United States, says Kananda, has inspired him with hopes for great possibilities in the future, but our destiny, as that of the world, rests not in the lawmakers of today, but in the women. Mr. Kananda's words: "The salvation of your country depends upon its women."

Buddhistic India

(Reproduced from the *Swami Vivekananda Centenary Memorial Volume*, published by the Swami Vivekananda Centenary, Calcutta, in 1963. The additions in square brackets have been made for purposes of clarification. Periods indicate probable omissions. — *Publisher*.)

(Delivered at the Shakespeare Club, Pasadena,
California, on February 2, 1900)

Buddhistic India is our subject tonight. Almost all of you, perhaps, have read Edwin Arnold's poem on the life of Buddha, and some of you, perhaps, have gone into the subject with more scholarly interest, as in English, French and German, there is quite a lot of Buddhistic literature. Buddhism itself is the most interesting of subjects, for it is the first historical outburst of a world religion. There have been great religions before Buddhism arose, in India and elsewhere, but, more or less, they are confined within their own races. The ancient Hindus or ancient Jews or ancient Persians, every one of them had a great religion, but these religions were more or less racial. With Buddhism first begins that peculiar phenomenon of religion boldly starting out to conquer the world. Apart from its doctrines and the truths it taught and the message it had to give, we stand face to face with one of the tremendous cataclysms of the world. Within a few centuries of its birth, the barefooted, shaven-headed missionaries of Buddha had spread over all the then known civilised world, and they penetrated even further — from Lapland on the one side to the Philippine Islands on the other. They had spread widely within a few centuries of Buddha's birth; and in India itself, the religion of Buddha had at one time nearly swallowed up two-thirds of the population.

The whole of India was never Buddhistic. It stood outside. Buddhism had the same fate as Christianity had with the Jews; the majority of the Jews stood aloof. So the old Indian religion lived on. But the comparison stops here. Christianity, though it could not get within its fold all the Jewish race, itself took the country. Where the old religion existed — the religion of the Jews — that was conquered by Christianity in a very short time and the old religion was dispersed, and so the religion of the Jews lives a sporadic life in different parts of the world. But in India this gigantic child was absorbed, in the long run, by the mother that gave it birth, and today the very name of Buddha is almost unknown all over India. You know more about Buddhism than ninety-nine per cent of the Indians. At best, they of India only know the name — "Oh, he was a great prophet, a great Incarnation of God" — and there it ends. The island of Ceylon remains to Buddha, and in some parts of the Himalayan country, there are some Buddhists yet. Beyond that there are none. But [Buddhism] has spread over all the rest of Asia.

Still, it has the largest number of followers of any religion, and it has indirectly modified the teachings of all the other religions. A good deal of Buddhism entered into Asia Minor. It was a constant fight at one time whether the Buddhists would prevail or the later sects of Christians. The [Gnostics] and the other sects of early Christians were more or less Buddhistic in their tendencies, and all these got fused up in that wonderful city of Alexandria, and out of the fusion under Roman law came Christianity. Buddhism in its political and social aspect is even more interesting than its [doctrines] and dogmas; and as the first outburst of the tremendous world-conquering power of religion, it is very interesting also.

I am mostly interested in this lecture in India as it has been affected by Buddhism; and to understand Buddhism and its rise a bit, we have to get a few ideas about India as it existed when this great prophet was born.

There was already in India a vast religion with an organised scripture — the Vedas; and these Vedas existed as a mass of literature and not a book — just as you find the Old Testament, the Bible. Now, the Bible is a mass of literature of different ages; different persons are the writers, and so on. It is a collection. Now, the Vedas are a vast collection. I do not know whether, if the texts were all found — nobody has found all the texts, nobody even in India has seen all the books — if all the books were known, this room would contain them. It is a huge mass of literature, carried down from generation to generation from God, who gave the scriptures. And the idea about the scriptures in India became tremendously orthodox. You complain of your orthodoxies in book-worship. If you get the Hindus' idea, where will you be? The Hindus think the Vedas are the direct knowledge of God, that God has created the whole universe in and through the Vedas, and that the whole universe exists because it is in the Vedas. The cow exists outside because the word "cow" is in the Vedas; man exists outside because of the word in the Vedas. Here you see the beginning of that theory which later on Christians developed and expressed in the text: "In the beginning was the Word and the Word was with God " It is the old, ancient theory of India. Upon that is based the whole idea of the scriptures. And mind, every word is the power of God. The word is only the external manifestation on the material plane. So, all this manifestation is just the manifestation on the material plane; and the Word is the Vedas, and Sanskrit is the language of God. God spoke once. He spoke in Sanskrit, and that is the divine language. Every other language, they consider, is no more than the braying of animals; and to denote that they call every other nation that does not speak Sanskrit [Mlechchhas], the same word as the barbarians of the Greeks. They are braying, not talking, and Sanskrit is the divine language.

Now, the Vedas were not written by anybody; they were eternally coexistent with God. God is infinite. So is knowledge, and through this knowledge is created the world. Their idea of ethics is [that a thing is good] because the law says so. Everything is bounded by that book — nothing [can go] beyond that, because the knowledge of God — you cannot get beyond that. That is Indian orthodoxy.

In the latter part of the Vedas, you see the highest, the spiritual. In the early portions, there is the crude part. You quote a passage from the Vedas — "That is not good", you say. "Why?" "There is a positive evil injunction" — the same as you see in the Old Testament. There are numbers of things in all old books, curious ideas, which we would not like in our present day. You say: "This doctrine is not at all good; why, it shocks my ethics!" How did you get your idea? [Merely] by your own thought? Get out! If it is ordained by God, what right have you to question? When the Vedas say, "Do not do this; this is immoral", and so on, no more have you the right to question at all. And that is the difficulty. If you tell a Hindu, "But our Bible does not say so", [he will reply] "Oh, your Bible! it is a babe of history. What other Bible could there be except the Vedas? What other book could there be? All knowledge is in God. Do you mean to say that He teaches by two or more Bibles? His knowledge came out in the Vedas. Do you mean to say that He committed a mistake, then? Afterwards, He wanted to do something better and taught another Bible to another nation? You cannot bring another book that is as old as Vedas. Everything else — it was all copied after that." They would not listen to you. And the Christian brings the Bible. They say: "That is fraud. God only speaks once, because He never makes mistakes."

Now, just think of that. That orthodoxy is terrible. And if you ask a Hindu that he is to reform his society and do this and that, he says: "Is it in the books? If it is not, I do not care to change. You wait. In five [hundred] years more you will find this is good." If you say to him, "This social institution that you have is not right", he says, "How do you know that?" Then he says: "Our social institutions in this matter are the better. Wait five [hundred] years and your institutions will die. The test is the survival of the fittest. You live, but there is not one community in the world which lives five hundred years together. Look here! We have been standing all the time." That is what they would say. Terrible orthodoxy! And thank God I have crossed that ocean.

This was the orthodoxy of India. What else was there? Everything was divided, the whole society, as it is today, though in a much more rigorous form then — divided into castes. There is another thing to learn. There is a tendency to make castes just [now] going on here in the West. And I myself — I am a renegade. I have broken everything. I do not believe in caste, individually. It has very good things in it. For myself, Lord help me! I would not have any caste, if He helps me. You understand what I mean by caste, and you are all trying to make it very fast. It is a hereditary trade [for] the Hindu. The Hindu said in olden times that life must be made easier and smoother. And what makes everything alive? Competition. Hereditary trade kills. You are a carpenter? Very good, your son can be only a carpenter. What are you? A blacksmith? Blacksmithing becomes a caste; your children will become blacksmiths. We do not allow anybody else to come into that trade, so you will be quiet and remain there. You are a military man, a fighter? Make a caste. You are a priest? Make a caste. The priesthood is hereditary. And so on. Rigid, high power! That has a great side, and that side is [that] it really rejects competition. It is that which has made the nation live while other nations have died — that caste. But there is a great evil: it checks individuality. I will have to be a carpenter because I am born a carpenter; but I do not like it. That is in the books, and that was before Buddha was born. I am talking to you of India as it was before Buddha. And you are trying today what you call socialism! Good things will come; but in the long run you will be a [blight] upon the race. Freedom is the watchword. Be free! A free body, a free mind, and a free soul! That is what I have felt all my life; I would rather be doing evil freely than be doing good under bondage.

Well, these things that they are crying for now in the West, they have done ages before there. Land has been nationalised . . . by thousands all these things. There is blame upon this hide-bound caste. The Indian people are intensely socialistic. But, beyond that, there is a wealth of individualism. They are as tremendously individualistic — that is to say, after laying down all these minute regulations. They have regulated how you should eat, drink, sleep, die! Everything is regulated there; from early morning to when you go to bed and sleep, you are following regulations and law. Law, law. Do you wonder that a nation should [live] under that? Law is death. The more of the law in a country, the worse for the country. [But to be an individual] we go to the mountains, where there is no law, no government. The more of law you make, the more of police and socialism, the more of blackguards there are. Now this tremendous regulation of law [is] there. As soon as a child is born, he knows that he is born a slave: slave to his caste, first; slave to his nation, next. Slave, slave, slave. Every action - his drinking and his eating. He must eat under a regular method; this prayer with the first morsel, this prayer with the second, that prayer with the third, and that prayer when he drinks water. Just think of that! Thus, from day to day, it goes on and on.

But they were thinkers. They knew that this would not lead to real greatness. So they left a way out for them all. After all, they found out that all these regulations are only for the world and the life of the world. As soon as you do not want money [and] you do not want children — no business for this world — you can go out entirely free. Those that go out thus were called Sannyasins — people who have given up. They never organised themselves, nor do they now; they are a free order of men and women who refuse to marry, who refuse to possess property, and they have no law — not even the Vedas bind them. They stand on [the] top of the Vedas. They are [at] the other pole [from] our social institutions. They are beyond caste. They have grown beyond. They are too big to be bound by these little regulations and things. Only two things [are] necessary for them: they must not possess property and must not marry. If you marry, settle down, or possess property, immediately the regulations will be upon you; but if you do not do either of these two, you are free. They were the living gods of the race, and ninety-nine per cent of our great men and women were to be found among them.

In every country, real greatness of the soul means extraordinary individuality, and that individuality you cannot get in society. It frets and fumes and wants to burst society. If society wants to keep it down, that soul wants to burst society into pieces. And they made an easy channel. They say: "Well, once you get out of society, then you may preach and teach everything that you like. We only worship you from a distance. So there were the tremendous, individualistic men and women, and they are the highest persons in all society. If one of those yellow-clad shaven-heads comes, the prince even dare not remain seated in his presence; he must stand. The next half hour, one of these Sannyasins might be at the door of one of the cottages of the poorest subjects, glad to get only a piece of bread. And he has to mix with all grades; now he sleeps with a poor man in his cottage; tomorrow [he] sleeps on the beautiful bed of a king. One day he dines on gold plates in kings' palaces; the next day, he has not any food and sleeps under a tree. Society looks upon these men with great respect; and some of them, just to show their individuality, will try to shock the public ideas. But the people are never shocked so long as they keep to these principles: perfect purity and no property.

These men, being very individualistic, they are always trying new theories and plans — visiting in every country. They must think something new; they cannot run in the old groove. Others are all trying to make us run in the old groove, forcing us all to think alike. But human nature is greater than any human foolishness. Our greatness is greater than our weakness; the good things are stronger than the evil things. Supposing they succeeded in making us all think in the same groove, there we would be — no more thought to think; we would die.

Here was a society which had almost no vitality, its members pressed down by iron chains of law. They were forced to help each other. There, one was under regulations [that were] tremendous: regulations even how to breathe: how to wash face and hands; how to bathe; how to brush the teeth; and so on, to the moment of death. And beyond these regulations was the wonderful individualism of the Sannyasin. There he was. And every days new sect was rising amongst these strong, individualistic men and women. The ancient Sanskrit books tell about their standing out — of one woman who was very quaint, queer old woman of the ancient times; she always had some new thing; sometimes [she was] criticised, but always people were afraid of her, obeying her quietly. So, there were those great men and women of olden times.

And within this society, so oppressed by regulations, the power was in the hands of the priests. In the social scale, the highest caste is [that of] the priest, and that being a business — I do not know any other word, that is why I use the word "priest". It is not in the same sense as in this country, because our priest is not a man that teaches religion or philosophy. The business of a priest is to perform all these minute details of regulations which have been laid down The priest is the man who helps in these regulations. He marries you; to your funeral he comes to pray. So at all the ceremonies performed upon a man or a woman, the priest must be there. In society the ideal is marriage. [Everyone] must marry. It is the rule. Without marriage, man is not able to perform any religious ceremony; he is only half a man; [he] is not competent to officiate — even the priest himself cannot officiate as a priest, except he marries. Half a man is unfit within society.

Now, the power of the priests increased tremendously. . . . The general policy of our national law-givers was to give the priests this honour. They also had the same socialistic plan [you are] just ready to [try] that checked them from getting money. What [was] the motive? Social honour. Mind you, the priest in all countries is the highest in the social scale, so much so in India that the poorest Brahmin is greater than the greatest king in the country, by birth. He is the nobleman in India. But the law does not allow him ever to become rich. The law grinds him down to poverty — only, it gives him this honour. He cannot do a thousand things; and the higher is the caste in the social scale, the more restricted are its enjoyments. The higher the caste, the less the number of kinds of food that man can eat, the less the amount of food that man may eat, the less the number of occupations [he may] engage in. To you, his life would be only a perpetual train of hardships — nothing more than that. It is a perpetual discipline in eating, drinking, and everything; and all [penalties] which are required from the lower caste are required from the higher ten times more. The lowest man tells a lie; his fine is one dollar. A Brahmin, he must pay, say, a hundred dollars — [for] he knows better.

But this was a grand organisation to start with. Later on, the time came when they, these priests, began to get all the power in their hands; and at last they forgot the secret of their power: poverty. They were men whom society fed and clad so that they might simply learn and teach and think. Instead of that, they began to spread out their hands to clutch at the riches of society. They became "money-grabbers" — to use your word — and forgot all these things.

Then there was the second caste, the kingly caste, the military. Actual power was in their hands. Not only so — they have produced all of our great thinkers, and not the Brahmins. It is curious. All our great prophets, almost without one exception, belong to the kingly caste. The great man Krishna was also of that caste; Rama, he also, and all our great philosophers, almost all [sat] on the throne; thence came all the great philosophers of renunciation. From the throne came the voice that always cried, "Renounce". These military people were their kings; and they [also] were the philosophers; they were the speakers in the Upanishads. In their brains and their thought, they were greater than the priests they were more powerful, they were the kings - and yet the priests got all the power and: tried to tyrannise over them. And so that was going on: political competition between the two castes, the priests and the kings.

Another phenomenon is there. Those of you that have been to hear the first lecture already know that in India there are two great races: one is called the Aryan; the other, the non-Aryan. It is the Aryan race that has the three castes; but the whole of the rest are dubbed with one name, Shudras — no caste. They are not Aryans at all. (Many people came from outside of India, and they found the Shudras [there], the aborigines of the country). However it may be, these vast masses of non-Aryan people and the mixed people among them, they gradually became civilised and they began to scheme for the same rights as the Aryans. They wanted to enter their schools and their colleges; they wanted to take the sacred thread of the Aryans; they wanted to perform the same ceremonies as the Aryans, and wanted to have equal rights in religion and politics like the Aryans. And the Brahmin priest, he was the great antagonist of such claims. You see, it is the nature of priests in every country — they are the most conservative people, naturally. So long as it is a trade, it must be; it is to their interest to be conservative. So this tide of murmur outside the Aryan pale, the priests were trying to check with all their might. Within the Aryan pale, there was also a tremendous religious ferment, and [it was] mostly led by this military caste.

There was already the sect of Jains [who are a] conservative [force] in India [even] today. It is a very ancient sect. They declared against the validity of the scriptures of the Hindus, the Vedas. They wrote some books themselves, and they said: "Our books are the only original books, the only original Vedas, and the Vedas that now are going on under that name have been written by the Brahmins to dupe the people." And they also laid the same plan. You see, it is difficult for you to meet the arguments of the Hindus about the scriptures. They also claimed [that] the world has been created through those books. And they were written in the popular language. The Sanskrit, even then, had ceased to be a spoken language — [it had] just the same relation [to the spoken language] as Latin has to modern Italian. Now, they wrote all their books in Pali; and when a Brahmin said, "Why, your books are in Pali! ", they said, "Sanskrit is a language of the dead."

In their methods and manners they were different. For, you see, these Hindu scriptures, the Vedas, are a vast mass of accumulation — some of them crude — until you come to where religion is taught, only the spiritual. Now, that was the portion of the Vedas which these sects all claimed to preach. Then, there are three steps in the ancient Vedas: first, work; second, worship; third, knowledge. When a man purifies himself by work and worship, then God is within that man. He has realised He is already there. He only can have seen Him because the mind has become pure. Now, the mind can become purified by work and worship. That is all. Salvation is already there. We don't know it. Therefore, work, worship, and knowledge are the three steps. By work, they mean doing good to others. That has, of course, something in it, but mostly, as to the Brahmins, work means to perform these elaborate ceremonials: killing of cows and killing of bulls, killing of goats and all sorts of animals, that are taken fresh and thrown into the fire, and so on. "Now" declared the Jains, "that is no work at all, because injuring others can never be any good work"; and they said; "This is the proof that your Vedas are false Vedas, manufactured by the priests, because you do not mean to say that any good book will order us [to be] killing animals and doing these things. You do not believe it. So all this killing of animals and other things that you see in the Vedas, they have been written by the Brahmins, because they alone are benefited. It is the priest only [who] pockets the money and goes home. So, therefore, it is all priest-craft."

It was one of their doctrines that there cannot be any God: "The priests have invented God, that the people may believe in God and pay them money. All nonsense! there is no God. There is nature and there are souls, and that is all. Souls have got entangled into this life and got round them the clothing of man you call a body. Now, do good work." But from that naturally came the doctrine that everything that is matter is vile. They are the first teachers of asceticism. If the body is the result of impurity, why, therefore the body is vile. If a man stands on one leg for some time — "All right, it is a punishment". If the head comes up bump against a wall — "Rejoice, it is a very good punishment". Some of the great founders of the [Franciscan Order] — one of them St. Francis — were going to a certain place to meet somebody; and St. Francis had one of his companions with him, and he began to talk as to whether [the person] would receive them or not, and this man suggested that possibly he would reject them. Said St. Francis: "That is not enough, brother, but if, when we go and knock at the door, the man comes and drives us away, that is not enough. But if he orders us to be bound and gives us a thorough whipping, even that is not enough. And then, if he binds us hand and foot and whips us until we bleed at every pore and throws us outside in the snow, that would be enough."

These [same] ascetic ideas prevailed at that time. These Jains were the first great ascetics; but they did some great work. "Don't injure any and do good to all that you can, and that is all the morality and ethics, and that is all the work there is, and the rest is all nonsense — the Brahmins created that. Throw it all away." And then they went to work and elaborated this one principle all through, and it is a most wonderful ideal: how all that we call ethics they simply bring out from that one great principle of non-injury and doing good.

This sect was at least five hundred years before Buddha, and he was five hundred and fifty years before Christ (The dates of the Jaina and Buddha were not known accurately in those days.). Now the whole of the animal creation they divide into five sections: the lowest have only one organ, that of touch; the next one, touch and taste; the next, touch, taste, and hearing; the next, touch, taste, hearing, and sight. And the next, the five organs. The first two, the one-organ and the two-organ, are invisible to the naked eye, and they art everywhere in water. A terrible thing, killing these [low forms of life]. This bacteriology has come into existence in the modern world only in the last twenty years and therefore nobody knew anything about it. They said, the lowest animals are only one-organ, touch; nothing else. The next greater [were] also invisible. And they all knew that if you boiled water these animals were ail killed. So these monks, if they died of thirst, they would never kill these animals by drinking water. But if [a monk] stands at your door and you give him a little boiled water, the sin is on you of killing the animals — and he will get the benefit. They carry these ideas to ludicrous extremes. For instance, in rubbing the body — if he bathes — he will have to kill numbers of animalcules; so he never bathes. He gets killed himself; he says that is all right. Life has no care for him; he will get killed and save life.

These Jains were there. There were various other sects of ascetics; and while this was going on, on the one hand, there was the political jealousy between the priests and the kings. And then these different dissatisfied sects [were] springing up everywhere. And there was the greater problem: the vast multitudes of people wanting the same rights as the Aryans, dying of thirst while the perennial stream of nature went flowing by them, and no right to drink a drop of water.

And that man was born — the great man Buddha. Most of you know about him, his life. And in spite of all the miracles and stories that generally get fastened upon any great man, in the first place, he is one of the most historical prophets of the world. Two are very historical: one, the most ancient, Buddha, and the other, Mohammed, because both friends and foes are agreed about them. So we are perfectly sure that there were such persons. As for the other persons, we have only to take for granted what the disciples say — nothing more. Our Krishna — you know, the Hindu prophet — he is very mythological. A good deal of his life, and everything about him, is written only by his disciples; and then there seem to be, sometimes, three or four men, who all loom into one. We do not know so clearly about many of the prophets; but as to this man, because both friends and foes write of him, we are sure that there was such a historical personage. And if we analyse through all the fables and reports of miracles and stories that generally are heaped upon a great man in this world, we will find an inside core; and all through the account of that man, he never did a thing for himself — never! How do you know that? Because, you see, when fables are fastened upon a man, the fables must be tinged with that man's general character. Not one fable tried to impute any vice or any immorality to the man. Even his enemies have favourable accounts.

When Buddha was born, he was so pure that whosoever looked at his face from a distance immediately gave up the ceremonial religion and became a monk and became saved. So the gods held a meeting. They said, "We are undone". Because most of the gods live upon the ceremonials. These sacrifices go to the gods and these sacrifices were all gone. The gods were dying of hunger and [the reason for] it was that their power was gone. So the gods said: "We must, anyhow, put this man down. He is too pure for our life." And then the gods came and said: "Sir, we come to ask you something. We want to make a great sacrifice and we mean to make a huge fire, and we have been seeking all over the world for a pure spot to light the fire on and could not find it, and now we have found it. If you will lie down, on your breast we will make the huge fire." "Granted," he says, "go on." And the gods built the fire high upon the breast of Buddha, and they thought he was dead, and he was not. And then they went about and said, "We are undone." And all the gods began to strike him. No good. They could not kill him. From underneath, the voice comes: "Why [are you] making all these vain attempts?" "Whoever looks upon you becomes purified and is saved, and nobody is going to worship us." "Then, your attempt is vain, because purity can never be killed." This fable was written by his enemies, and yet throughout the fable the only blame that attaches to Buddha is that he was so great a teacher of purity.

About his doctrines, some of you know a little. It is his doctrines that appeal to many modern thinkers whom you call agnostics He was a great preacher of the brotherhood of mankind: "Aryan or non-Aryan, caste or no caste, and sects or no sects, every one has the same right to God and to religion and to freedom. Come in all of you." But as to other things, he was very agnostic. "Be practical." There came to him one day five young men, Brahmin born, quarrelling upon a question. They came to him to ask him the way to truth. And one said: "My people teach this, and this is the way to truth." The other said: "I have been taught this, and this is the only way to truth." "Which is the right way, sir?" "Well, you say your people taught this is truth and is the way to God?" "Yes." "But did you see God?" "No, sir." "Your father?" "No, sir." "Your grandfather?" "No, sir." "None of them saw God?" "No" "Well, and your teachers — neither [any] of them saw God?" "No." And he asked the same to the others. They all declared that none had seen God. "Well," said Buddha, "in a certain village came a young man weeping and howling and crying: 'Oh, I love her so! oh my, I love her so!' And then the villagers came; and the only thing he said was he loved her so. 'Who is she that you love?' 'I do not know.' 'Where does she live?' 'I do not know' — but he loved her so. 'How does she look?' 'That I do not know; but oh, I love her so.'" Then asked Buddha: "Young man, what would you call this young man?" "Why, sir, he was a fool!" And they all declared: "Why, sir, that young man was certainly a fool, to be crying and all that about a woman, to say he loved her so much and he never saw her or knew that she existed or anything?" "Are you not the same? You say that this God your father or your grandfather never saw, and now you are quarrelling upon a thing which neither you nor your ancestors ever knew, and you are trying to cut each other's throats about it." Then the young men asked: "What are we to do?" "Now, tell me: did your father ever teach that God is ever angry?" "No, sir." "Did your father ever teach that God is evil?" "No, sir, He is always pure." "Well, now, if you are pure and good and all that, do you not think that you will have more chance to come near to that God than by discussing all this and trying to cut each other's throats? Therefore, say I: be pure and be good; be pure and love everyone." And that was [all].

You see that non-killing of animals and charity towards animals was an already existing doctrine when he was born; but it was new with him — the breaking down of caste, that tremendous movement. And the other thing that was new: he took forty of his disciples and sent them all over the world, saying, "Go ye; mix with all races and nations and preach the excellent gospel for the good of all, for the benefit of all." And, of course, he was not molested by the Hindus. He died at a ripe old age. All his life he was a most stern man: he never yielded to weakness. I do not believe many of his doctrines; of course, I do not. I believe that the Vedantism of the old Hindus is much more thoughtful, is a grander philosophy of life. I like his method of work, but what I like [most] in that man is that, among all the prophets of mankind, here was a man who never had any cobwebs in his brain, and [who was] sane and strong. When kingdoms were at his feet, he was still the same man, maintaining "I am a man amongst men."

Why, the Hindus, they are dying to worship somebody. You will find, if you live long enough, I will be worshipped by our people. If you go there to teach them something, before you die you will be worshipped. Always trying to worship somebody. And living in that race, the world-honoured Buddha, he died always declaring that he was but man. None of his adulators could draw from him one remark that he was anything different from any other man.

Those last dying words of his always thrilled through my heart. He was old, he was suffering, he was near his death, and then came the despised outcaste — he lives on carrion, dead animals; the Hindus would not allow them to come into cities — one of these invited him to a dinner and he came with his disciples, and the poor Chanda, he wanted to treat this great teacher according to what he thought would be best; so he had a lot of pig's flesh and a lot of rice for him, and Buddha looked at that. The disciples were all [hesitating], and the Master said: "Well, do not eat, you will be hurt." But he quietly sat down and ate. The teacher of equality must eat the [outcaste] Chanda's dinner, even the pig's flesh. He sat down and ate it.

He was already dying. He found death coming on, and he asked, "Spread for me something under this tree, for I think the end is near." And he was there under the tree, and he laid himself down; he could not sit up any more. And the first thing he did, he said: "Go to that Chanda and tell him that he has been one of my greatest benefactors; for his meal, I am going to Nirvâna." And then several men came to be instructed, and a disciple said, "Do not go near now, the Master is passing away". And as soon as he heard it, the Lord said, "Let them come in". And somebody else came and the disciples would not [let them enter]. Again they came, and then the dying Lord said: "And O, thou Ananda, I am passing away. Weep not for me. Think not for me. I am gone. Work out diligently your own salvation. Each one of you is just what I am. I am nothing but one of you. What I am today is what I made myself. Do you struggle and make yourselves what I am. . . ."

These are the memorable words of Buddha: "Believe not because an old book is produced as an authority. Believe not because your father said [you should] believe the same. Believe not because other people like you believe it. Test everything, try everything, and then believe it, and if you find it for the good of many, give it to all." And with these words, the Master passed away.

See the sanity of the man. No gods, no angels, no demons — nobody. Nothing of the kind. Stern, sane, every brain-cell perfect and complete, even at the moment of death. No delusion. I do not agree with many of his doctrines. You may not. But in my opinion — oh, if I had only one drop of that strength! The sanest philosopher the world ever saw. Its best and its sanest teacher. And never that man bent before even the power of the tyrannical Brahmins. Never that man bent. Direct and everywhere the same: weeping with the miserable, helping the miserable, singing with the singing, strong with the strong, and everywhere the same sane and able man.

And, of course, with all this I can [not] understand his doctrine. You know he denied that there was any soul in man — that is, in the Hindu sense of the word. Now, we Hindus all believe that there is something permanent in man, which is unchangeable and which is living through all eternity. And that in man we call Atman, which is without beginning and without end. And [we believe] that there is something permanent in nature [and that we call Brahman, which is also without beginning and without end]. He denied both of these. He said there is no proof of anything permanent. It is all a mere mass of change; a mass of thought in a continuous change is what you call a mind. ... The torch is leading the procession. The circle is a delusion. [Or take the example of a river.] It is a continuous river passing on; every moment a fresh mass of water passing on. So is this life; so is all body, so is all mind.

Well, I do not understand his doctrine — we Hindus never understood it. But I can understand the motive behind that. Oh, the gigantic motive! The Master says that selfishness is the great curse of the world; that we are selfish and that therein is the curse. There should be no motive for selfishness. You are [like a river] passing [on] — a continuous phenomenon. Have no God; have no soul; stand on your feet and do good for good's sake — neither for fear of punishment nor for [the sake of] going anywhere. Stand sane and motiveless. The motive is: I want to do good, it is good to do good. Tremendous! Tremendous! I do not sympathise with his metaphysics at all; but my mind is jealous when I think of the moral force. Just ask your minds which one of you can stand for one hour, able and daring like that man. I cannot for five minutes. I would become a coward and want a support. I am weak — a coward. And I warm to think of this tremendous giant. We cannot approach that strength. The world never saw [anything] compared to that strength. And I have not yet seen any other strength like that. We are all born cowards. If we can save ourselves [we care about nothing else]. Inside is the tremendous fear, the tremendous motive, all the time. Our own selfishness makes us the most arrant cowards; our own selfishness is the great cause of fear and cowardice. And there he stood: "Do good because it is good; ask no more questions; that is enough. A man made to do good by a fable, a story, a superstition — he will be doing evil as soon as the opportunity comes. That man alone is good who does good for good's sake, and that is the character of the man."

"And what remains of man?" was asked of the Master. "Everything — everything. But what is in the man? Not the body not the soul, but character. And that is left for all ages. All that have passed and died, they have left for us their characters, eternal possessions for the rest of humanity; and these characters are working — working all through." What of Buddha? What of Jesus of Nazareth? The world is full of their characters. Tremendous doctrine!

Let us come down a little — we have not come to the subject at all. (*Laughter.*) I must add not a few words more this evening. ...

And then, what he did. His method of work: organisation. The idea that you have today of church is his character. He left the church. He organised these monks and made them into a body. Even the voting by ballot is there five hundred and sixty years before Christ. Minute organization. The church was left and became a tremendous power, and did great missionary work in India and outside India. Then came, three hundred years after, two hundred years before Christ, the great emperor Asoka, as he has been called by your Western historians, the divinest of monarchs, and that man became entirely converted to the ideas of Buddha, and he was the greatest emperor of the world at that time. His grandfather was a contemporary of Alexander, and since Alexander's time, India had become more intimately connected with Greece. ... Every day in Central Asia some inscription or other is being found. India had forgotten all about Buddha and Asoka and everyone. But there were pillars, obelisks, columns, with ancient letters which nobody could read. Some of the old Mogul emperors declared they would give millions for anybody to read those; but nobody could. Within the last thirty years those have been read; they are all written in Pali.

The first inscription is: "..."

And then he writes this inscription, describing the terror and the misery of war; and then he became converted to religion. Then said he: "Henceforth let none of my descendants think of acquiring glory by conquering other races. If they want glory, let them help other races; let them send teachers of sciences and teachers of religion. A glory won by the sword is no glory at all." And next you find how he is sending missionaries even to Alexandria.... You wonder that you find all over that part of the country sects rising immediately, called Theraputae, Essenes, and all those — extreme vegetarians, and so on. Now this great Emperor Asoka built hospitals for men and for animals. The inscriptions show they are ordering hospitals, building hospitals for men and for animals. That is to say, when an animal gets old, if I am poor and cannot keep it any longer, I do not shoot it down for mercy. These hospitals are maintained by public charity. The coasting traders pay so much upon every hundredweight they sell, and all that goes to the hospital; so nobody is touched. If you have a cow that is old — anything — and do not want to keep it, send it to the hospital; they keep it, even down to rats and mice and anything you send. Only, our ladies try to kill these animals sometimes, you know. They go in large numbers to see them and they bring all sorts of cakes; the animals are killed many times by this food. He claimed that the animals should be as much under the protection of the government as man. Why should animals be allowed to be killed? [There] is no reason. But he says, before prohibiting the killing of animals for food even, [people] must be provided with all sorts of vegetables. So he sent and collected all kinds of vegetables and planted them in India; and then, as soon as these were introduced, the order was: henceforth, whosoever kills an animal will be punished. A government is to be a government; the animals must be protected also. What business has a man to kill a cow, a goat, or any other animal for food?

Thus Buddhism was and did become a great political power in India. Gradually it also fell to pieces — after all, this tremendous missionary enterprise. But to their credit it must be said, they never took up the sword to preach religion. Excepting the Buddhistic religion, there is not one

religion in the world which could make one step without bloodshed —
not one which could get a hundred thousand converts just by brain power
alone. No, no. All through. And this is just what you are going to do in the
Philippines. That is your method. Make them religious by the sword. That
is what your priests are preaching. Conquer and kill them that they may get
religion. A wonderful way of preaching religion!

You know how this great emperor Asoka was converted. This great
emperor in his youth was not so good. [He had a brother.] And the two
brothers quarrelled and the other brother defeated this one, and the emperor
in vengeance wanted to kill him. The emperor got the news that he had
taken shelter with a Buddhistic monk. Now, I have told you how our monks
are very holy; no one would come near them. The emperor himself came. He
said, "Deliver the man to me" Then the monk preached to him: "Vengeance
is bad. Disarm anger with love. Anger is not cured by anger, nor hatred by
hatred. Dissolve anger by love. Cure hatred by love. Friend, if for one evil
thou returnest another, thou curest not the first evil, but only add one evil
more to the world." The emperor said: "That is all right, fool that you are.
Are you ready to give your life — to give your life for that man?" "Ready,
sir." And he came out. And the emperor drew his sword, and he said: "Get
ready." And just [as he] was going to strike, he looked at the face of the man.
There was not a wink in those eyes. The emperor stopped, and he said: "Tell
me, monk, where did you learn this strength, poor beggar, not to wink?"
And then he preached again. "Go on, monk", he said, "That is nice", he said.
Accordingly, he [fell under] the charm of the Master — Buddha's charm.

There have been three things in Buddhism: the Buddha himself, his law,
his church. At first it was so simple. When the Master died, before his death,
they said: "What shall we do with you?" "Nothing." "What monuments
shall we make over you?" He said: "Just make a little heap if you want,
or just do not do anything." By and by, there arose huge temples and all
the paraphernalia. The use of images was unknown before then. I say they
were the first to use images. There are images of Buddha and all the saints,
sitting about and praying. All this paraphernalia went on multiplying with
this organisation. Then these monasteries became rich. The real cause of
the downfall is here. Monasticism is all very good for a few; but when
you preach it in such a fashion that every man or woman who has a mind
immediately gives up social life, when you find over the whole of India
monasteries, some containing a hundred thousand monks, sometimes
twenty thousand monks in one building — huge, gigantic buildings, these
monasteries, scattered all over India and, of course, centres of learning, and
all that — who were left to procreate progeny, to continue the race? Only

the weaklings. All the strong and vigorous minds went out. And then came national decay by the sheer loss of vigour.

I will tell you of this marvellous brotherhood. It is great. But theory and idea is one thing and actual working is another thing. The idea is very great: practicing nonresistance and all that, but if all of us go out in the street and practice non-resistance, there would be very little left in this city. That is to say, the idea is all right, but nobody has yet found a practical solution [as to] how to attain it.

There is something in caste, so far as it means blood; such a thing as heredity there is, certainly. Now try to [understand] — why do you not mix your blood with the Negroes, the American Indians? Nature will not allow you. Nature does not allow you to mix your blood with them. There is the unconscious working that saves the race. That was the Aryan's caste. Mind you, I do not say that they are not equal to us. They must have the same privileges and advantages, and everything; but we know that if certain races mix up, they become degraded. With all the strict caste of the Aryan and non-Aryan, that wall was thrown down to a certain extent, and hordes of these outlandish races came in with all their queer superstitions and manners and customs. Think of this: not decency enough to wear clothes, eating carrion, etc. But behind him came his fetish, his human sacrifice, his superstition, his diabolism. He kept it behind, [he remained] decent for a few years. After that he brought all [these] things out in front. And that was degrading to the whole race. And then the blood mixed; [intermarriages] took place with all sorts of unmixable races. The race fell down. But, in the long run it proved good. If you mix up with Negroes and American Indians, surely this civilisation will fall down. But hundreds and hundreds years after, out of this mixture will come a gigantic race once more, stronger than ever; but, for the time being, you have to suffer. The Hindus believe — that is a peculiar belief, I think; and I do not know, I have nothing to say to the contrary, I have not found anything to the contrary — they believe there was only one civilised race: the Aryan. Until he gives his blood, no other race can be civilised. No teaching will do. The Aryan gives his blood to a race, and then it becomes civilised. Teaching alone will not do. He would be an example in your country: would you give your blood to the Negro race? Then he would get higher culture.

The Hindu loves caste. I may have little taint of that superstition — I do not know. I love the Master's ideal. Great! But, for me, I do not think that the working was very practical; and that was one of the great causes that led to the downfall of the Indian nation, in the long run. But then it brought about this tremendous fusion. Where so many different races are all fusing, mingling — one man white like you, or yellow, while another man as black as I am, and all grades between these two extremes, and each race keeping their customs, manners, and everything — in the long run a fusion is taking place, and out of this fusion surely will come a tremendous upheaval; but, for the time being, the giant must sleep. That is the effect of all such fusion.

When Buddhism went down that way, there came they inevitable reaction. There is but one entity in the wholes world. It is a unit world. The diversity is only eye-service. It is all one. The idea of unity and what we call monism — without duality — is the idea in India. This doctrine has: been always in India; [it was] brought forward whenever materialism and scepticism broke down everything. When Buddhism broke down everything by introducing all sorts of foreign barbarians into India — their manners and customs and things — there was a reaction, and that reaction was led by a young monk [Shankarâchârya]. And [instead] of preaching new doctrines and always thinking new thoughts and making sects, he brought back the Vedas to life: and modern Hinduism has thus an admixture of ancient Hinduism, over which the Vedantists predominate. But, you see, what once dies never comes back to life, and those ceremonials of [Hinduism] never came back to life. You will be astonished if I tell you that, according to the old ceremonials, he is not a good Hindu who does not eat beef. On certain occasions he must sacrifice a bull and eat it. That is disgusting now. However they may differ from each other in India, in that they are all one — they never eat beef. The ancient sacrifices and the ancient gods, they are all gone; modern India belongs to the spiritual part of the Vedas.

Buddhism was the first sect in India. They were the first to say: "Ours is the only path. Until you join our church, you cannot be saved." That was what they said: "It is the correct path." But, being of Hindu blood, they could not be such stony-hearted sectarians as in other countries. There will be salvation for you: nobody will go wrong for ever. No, no. [There was] too much of Hindu blood in them for that. The heart was not so stony as that. But you have to join them.

But the Hindu idea, you know, is not to join anybody. Wherever you are, that is a point from which you can start to the centre. All right. It — Hinduism — has this advantage: its secret is that doctrines and dogmas do not mean anything; what you are is what matters. If you talk all the best philosophies the world ever produced, [but] if you are a fool in your behaviour, they do not count; and if in your behaviour you are good, you have more chances. This being so, the Vedantist can wait for everybody. Vedantism teaches that there is but one existence and one thing real, and that is God. It is beyond all time and space and causation and everything. We can never define Him. We can never say what He is except [that] He is Absolute Existence, Absolute Knowledge, Absolute Blissfulness. He is the only reality. Of everything He is the reality; of you and me, of the wall and of [everything] everywhere. It is His knowledge upon which all our knowledge depends: it is His blissfulness upon which depends our pleasure; and He is the only reality. And when man realises this, he knows that "I am the only reality, because I am He — what is real in me is He also". So that when a man is perfectly pure and good and beyond all grossness, he finds, as Jesus found: "I and my Father are one." The Vedantist has patience to wait for everybody. Wherever you are, this is the highest: "I and my Father are one." Realise it. If an image helps, images are welcome. If worshipping a great man helps you, worship him. If worshipping Mohammed helps you, go on. Only be sincere; and if you are sincere, says Vedantism, you are sure to be brought to the goal. None will be left. your heart, which contains all truth, will unfold itself chapter after chapter, till you know the last truth, that "I and my Father are one". And what is salvation? To live with God. Where? Anywhere. Here this moment. One moment in infinite time is quite as good as any other moment. This is the old doctrine of the Vedas, you see. This was revived. Buddhism died out of India. It left its mark on their charity, its animals, etc. in India; and Vedantism is reconquering India from one end to the other.